Sign Language & Body Parts

Bela Davis

Abdo Kids Junior
is an Imprint of Abdo Kids
abdobooks.com

Abdo
EVERYDAY SIGN LANGUAGE
Kids

abdobooks.com

Published by Abdo Kids, a division of ABDO, P.O. Box 398166, Minneapolis, Minnesota 55439. Copyright © 2023 by Abdo Consulting Group, Inc. International copyrights reserved in all countries. No part of this book may be reproduced in any form without written permission from the publisher. Abdo Kids Junior™ is a trademark and logo of Abdo Kids.

Printed in the United States of America, North Mankato, Minnesota.

102022

012023

THIS BOOK CONTAINS RECYCLED MATERIALS

Photo Credits: Shutterstock

Production Contributors: Teddy Borth, Jennie Forsberg, Grace Hansen

Design Contributors: Candice Keimig, Pakou Moua

Library of Congress Control Number: 2022937170

Publisher's Cataloging-in-Publication Data

Names: Davis, Bela, author.

Title: Sign language & body parts / by Bela Davis

Description: Minneapolis, Minnesota : Abdo Kids, 2023 | Series: Everyday sign language | Includes online resources and index.

Identifiers: ISBN 9781098264062 (lib. bdg.) | ISBN 9781098264628 (ebook) | ISBN 9781098264901 (Read-to-Me ebook)

Subjects: LCSH: American Sign Language--Juvenile literature. | Human anatomy--Juvenile literature. | Deaf--Means of communication--Juvenile literature. | Language acquisition--Juvenile literature.

Classification: DDC 419--dc23

Table of Contents

Signs and Body Parts

ASL is a visual language. There is a sign for all the body parts!

foot

BODY

1. Make the "B" sign with both hands
2. Place hands on the shoulders, palms facing in
3. Bring hands down in a semi-circle, ending at hips with palms still facing in

leg

arm

Eva dances to the music. She waves her arms in the air.

ARM

1. Hold the non-dominant arm out in front of the body, palm facing down

2. Make the "B" sign with the dominant hand

3. Bring the "B" sign to the opposite shoulder and slide it down toward the wrist

7

Abby holds a balloon

in her hand.

HAND

1. Hold up both hands with fingers stuck together and palms facing in

2. Take the dominant hand's fingertips and slide them from the wrist to the fingertips of the non-dominant hand

3. To say "hands" repeat this motion with the other hand

Martin stands on one leg.

He is good at **balancing**.

LEG

1. Using the dominant hand, tuck in all fingers except for the index finger

2. Point up and down one leg by starting at the hip and moving down toward the leg, and back up

Josh likes to play soccer.
He can kick the ball with
both feet.

FEET

1. Using the dominant hand, tuck in all fingers except for the index finger

2. Point in the direction of one foot and then the other

13

It is Tessa's birthday!

She wears a party hat
on her head.

HEAD

1. Using the dominant hand, bend the fingers at the large knuckles

2. Touch the fingertips to the temple, palm facing down

3. Then touch the fingertips to the chin

Something smells!

Ian plugs his nose.

NOSE

1. Using the dominant hand, tuck in all fingers except for the index finger

2. Simply point toward the nose or tap on it

17

Dan loved science class today. He learned about how the ear works.

EAR

1. Using the dominant hand, tuck in all fingers except for the index finger
2. Simply point toward the ear
3. Or grab the earlobe and wiggle it

Alma's glasses help
her eyes see better!

EYE

1. Using the dominant hand, tuck in all fingers except for the index finger

2. Point toward the eye

21

The ASL Alphabet!

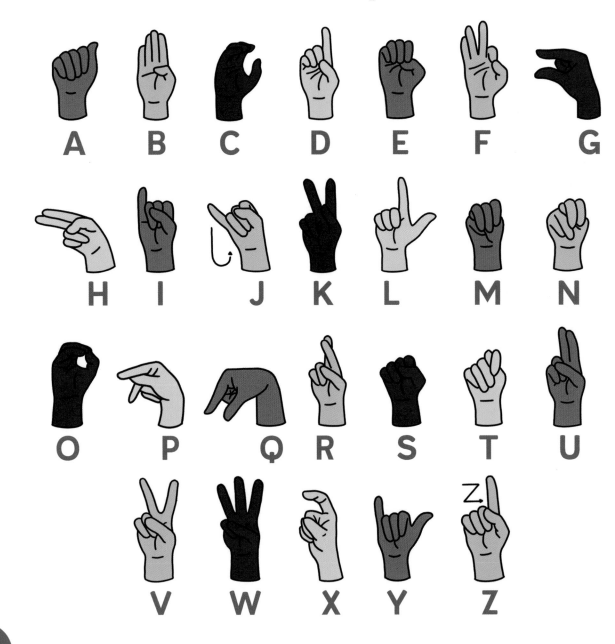

Glossary

ASL
short for American Sign Language, a language used by many deaf people in North America.

balancing
holding steady.

23

Index

Abdo Kids
ONLINE
FREE! ONLINE MULTIMEDIA RESOURCES

Visit **abdokids.com** to access crafts, games, videos, and more!

Use Abdo Kids code
ESK4062
or scan this QR code!